Old Anderston and Finniesto

by Guthrie Hutton

Stobcross Motor Garage was one of many in the Finnieston area which has been used for making and mending cars since the dawn of the automotive age.

First published in the United Kingdom, 2007,
by Stenlake Publishing Ltd.
www.stenlake.co.uk
ISBN 9781840333930

The publishers regret that they cannot supply copies of any pictures featured in this book.

A Parliamentary Act of 1863 authorised civil authorities to establish local libraries, but attempts to persuade Glasgow ratepayers to accept the additional cost failed until the necessary provisions were included in a catch-all Tramway and General Purposes Act, in 1899. Anderston District Library was the city's third local library, opened in December 1904. It was built to the designs of architects Stewart & Paterson and included a lending facility, general reference room, and reading rooms for ladies and children. Closed in 1969 as part of the area redevelopment, its services were transferred to the Mitchell Library building with an entrance off Berkeley Street.

Acknowledgments

I would like to thank a number of people who helped me to compile this story. David McLaughlin provided a couple of pictures and gave me some interesting quotes, especially the one about 'USA'. Iain Hogg, who has an impeccable claim to the USA tag, provided some useful anecdotes. Douglas Leitch, who played his part in the story, added more, as did my old friend Tommy Lawton, who also came up with a cracking picture. Sandra Reid supplied a remarkable picture, and superb pictures also came from colleagues in the world of local history publishing, Neil Parkhouse, Robert Grieves and W. A. C. Smith. David Warrillow provided some splendid pictures and a barrow load of banter, and Douglas Annan of T. & R. Annan agreed to my use of the picture on page 4. John Goudie, President of the St Vincent Bowling Club, let me use the picture on page 42. The picture on page 45 came from the Royal Commission for the Ancient and Historical Monuments of Scotland. They all made it possible and I am indebted to them all.

Further Reading

The books listed below were used by the author during his research. None are available from Stenlake Publishing; please contact your local bookshop or reference library.

Cooper, John N., *Simply Anderston*, 1972.
Cowan, James, *From Glasgow's Treasure Chest*, 1951.
Glenday, David, *Anderston As It Was, 1992*, reprinted 1994.
Henderson, Thomas, *The Savings Bank of Glasgow 1836–1936*, 1936.
Hume, John R., *Industrial Archaeology of Glasgow*, 1974.
Leask, Douglas P., *A Century of Bowling 1859–1959* (booklet).
Peter, Bruce, *100 Years of Glasgow's Amazing Cinemas*, c.1996.
Riddell, John F., *Clyde Navigation*, 1979.
Roxburgh, James M., *The School Board of Glasgow 1873–1919*, 1971.
Smart, Aileen, *Villages of Glasgow*, Volume 1, 1988.
Williamson, Elizabeth et al., *The Buildings of Scotland: Glasgow*, 1990.

Introduction

The village of Andersonstown, later shortened to Anderston, began in 1725 when James Anderson feued out an unproductive part of his Stobcross Estate for the building of weavers' cottages. It grew slowly, but when John Orr, a merchant from the Barrowfield (Bridgeton) area, bought the estate in 1735 the pace quickened. To weaving was added dyeing and bleaching, but soon hand-made linen was being ousted by cotton woven on large steam-driven looms. Other industries, like pottery, brewing and glassmaking, became established and reservoirs were sited on high ground at Cranstonhill.

Anderston achieved sufficient size and status to become a separate burgh in 1824 with the principal cotton master, Henry Houldsworth, as its first provost. Glasgow was also growing, and if the good folk of Anderston thought burghal status would ensure independence they were disappointed in 1846 when their infant burgh was absorbed into the city – probably the shortest-lived burgh in Scottish history.

As heavy industry supplanted cotton and shipping developed on the Clyde, the streets close to the riverside became warrens of works and warehouses, making and storing things for ships and the sea. Anderston spread westward across Cranstonhill and Stobcross to Finnieston, a small community named after the Reverend John Finnie, the Orr family tutor. There weavers' cottages were soon replaced by fine housing as Finnieston grew into an upmarket suburb, and just as quickly lost its appeal when docks and railways filled the parkland beside the Clyde. By the close of the nineteenth century, shipping and associated industries had become the settled activity of a large area characterised by back-street and back-court workshops, and densely populated closely packed tenements.

Glasgow peaked commercially just before the First World War and decline continued into the 1950s when, in the wake of another world war, people decided that the city needed regeneration. Certainly many old buildings were in a dire state of repair and sanitary conditions in some were dreadful, but the remedy was drastic as whole areas, including Anderston, were identified for wholesale redevelopment. Allied to this was the city's other grand plan – a network of fast roads designed to speed traffic through, round and into the city – and its implementation meant that much of Anderston disappeared to make way for the concrete and tarmac of the M8 motorway and Clydeside Expressway. At the same time block after block of tenement streets were torn down in an orgy of demolition inspired by a planners' dream that became a nightmare.

Few districts of Glasgow were so completely cleared in the 1960s and 70s, but the impact of what happened was compounded because the world was also changing, and no industry reflected this more than shipping. Containerisation (developed in the 1950s) was growing rapidly, bulk carrying was increasing, shipbuilding on the Clyde was declining and air travel was becoming commonplace, all of which rendered Glasgow's docks obsolete within a shockingly quick time-scale. So no sooner had Anderston been knocked down than its industry disappeared and the area became empty and derelict. Now, decades after demolition, the riverside has started to recover, but the life and vibrancy the city planners tore out of the heart of the old burgh area has not yet returned, and displaced former residents, with defiant cynicism, still say they are from the USA – 'Used to Stay in Anderston'!

The Finnieston Ferry framed by a crane on Stobcross Quay.

Anderston Cross was a busy junction graced by this splendid keynote building at the gushet of Argyle and Stobcross Streets. The two-storey part of the structure, on the left of the picture, was the entrance to the station. It was on the Caledonian Railway Company's Glasgow Central Railway which ran underground for most of its route between Maryhill and Dalmarnock. Although the station was below street level it had a vent behind the building to allow fresh air into the platforms, and smoke and steam to escape.

These modern views show what replaced the buildings on the facing page when Anderston Cross was demolished. The upper picture was taken from as near as possible to the same angle. The only link to the old view is the modern, less impressive, station entrance in the gloom below the motorway carriageways. The lower picture looks east, towards the city. It was taken from a pedestrian bridge over the Stobcross Street section of the Clydeside Expressway. The only thing remaining from the original structures is the station vent - the large hole in the centre of the picture with the heavy retaining wall on the left. The new station entrance can be seen beyond it, tucked in below the motorway. The five-storey part of the Anderston Cross building would have been to the left of the new station, rising to the height of the motorway ramp in front of the Marriot Hotel. The towers of the Anderston Centre can be seen beyond the hotel. Amost hidden behind the flyovers on the right is Washington Street School, which was effectively brought closer to Argyle Street when a run of tenements, seen on page 9, was demolished and the street widened to lead onto the Expressway.

Glasgow's civic leaders were proud of their plans to replace soot-blackened tenements with clean-lined, futuristic-looking developments like the Anderston Centre. It was intended as a 'decked commercial zone' with car parking and a bus station at street level, shops and supermarkets above, and housing on the upper floors, but the dream quickly faded as the shops and even the bus station closed. Part of the hoarding containing the site is seen on the left of this picture of a Corporation bus heading west along Argyle Street in 1966. The picture is actually on the city side of the old burgh boundary as indeed was most of the Anderston Centre, but whatever its name, it would have fared the same, a failure to match expectations that had a lot to do with its being too far out of the city centre. This experience suggests that the prediction of the seventeenth-century prophet, Alexander Peden, that 'the Cross of Glasgow would one day stand at the Hillhead of Stobcross', has still got a wee while to wait before it comes to fruition.

Peden's vision was brutally thwarted by the planners of the 1950s and 60s who bounded the city centre with the M8 motorway, and also gave today's planners the problem of how to get development to jump the barrier it has created. The motorway was originally planned as an inner ring road encircling the city, but only the northern and western half was built, carving a route through Townhead and Charing Cross before crossing the Clyde between Anderston and Kingston on the largest urban bridge built at that time. Known as the Kingston Bridge (why not Anderston Bridge?) there was enormous pride when it was opened by Queen Elizabeth, the Queen Mother, in June 1970. Failure to complete the ring, and the huge increase in road traffic, has, however, placed a much heavier burden on the structure than was initially anticipated, resulting in structural problems and lane restrictions. The bridge is seen here during construction.

A hand-written note on the back of this picture describes it as 'Anderston Cross forty years ago'. It is dated 1904, implying that it shows the cross in 1864, but while that is probably too precise, it does give some indication of the picture's age. It is also difficult to be certain about what it shows. The sunlit buildings and direction of the shadows suggest it could be on the north side of Main Street, and the horse buses are pointing in the direction of the city as they wait for passengers. The buses, which ran between Anderston Cross and Glasgow Cross, belonged to rival companies, that of Duncan McGregor in the centre of the picture and Andrew Menzies on the right. Both painted their vehicles in their tartans. This clan battle appears to have been won by Andrew Menzies, who kept his large fleet of buses, and hundreds of horses, in North Street. His operating expertise was also recognised when trams superseded the buses, because he became managing director of the new company.

The name of Main Street, Anderston, was changed to Argyle Street in 1906 to avoid confusion with the many other Main Streets in villages taken over by Glasgow. This picture, which shows Argyle Street looking east from Anderston Cross, with Stobcross Street joining from the right, could be of the same section of road shown on the facing page if the earlier picture of Main Street has been identified correctly. Redevelopment in the second half of the nineteenth century has of course physically transformed the scene, but it could be that the trams are occupying a similar position to the horse buses. The picture is tricky to date with precision, but is thought to be from the 1920s and is one of twelve old postcards in this book that were printed in a fuzzy way for artistic effect. This deliberate diminution of clarity is irksome, but the images of long-demolished scenes are, nonetheless, priceless.

With Stobcross Street on the left and Argyle Street on the right, the Anderston Cross building exemplified the confident verve with which Glasgow's Victorian architects tackled such prominent sites. Designed by J. J. Burnet at the time of the railway's construction in the 1890s, its towering chimney heads, frontal gables, glazed studio roof, balustrades and other detailed stonework made it a highly distinctive structure. Such splendour, alas, failed to move the road planners of the 1960s and, as they plotted the building's downfall, it was allowed to deteriorate, losing its gloss and its glass roof before being demolished in 1967. A decade later, a little book about Glasgow's trams published a similar view with a caption which began: 'It took some detective work to determine just where this was . . .'. In all probability the writer knew what the picture showed and used the words as a device to show that by that time Anderston Cross had been wiped from the face of the earth and nothing remained to remind people of what it once looked like.

In this view of Anderston Cross the photographer has moved round to favour Argyle Street, with the central gushet building on the left. As ever, there is a tram in the picture. Horse-drawn trams started to operate in the city in 1872 under a private company, the Glasgow Tramway and Omnibus Company (G. T. & O.), although Glasgow Corporation laid and maintained the track and also ran about half the trams as the system expanded. When the G. T. & O.'s lease expired in 1894, the Corporation took over the running of all trams and, between 1898 and 1902, electrified the system. Argyle Street seemed to be the natural home of the 'caurs', with a never-ending stream of them rattling along from morning to night. The tram numbered 91, seen here heading for the city, was introduced to the system in 1920. It is about to pass the three-storey building on the right where the Brown Brothers' hat shop was on the first floor and Mrs John Mill had a boot and shoe shop on the ground-floor corner with Bishop Street.

Anderston Cross Station, seen here in 1959, was grander above ground than it was at platform level, but the below-street-level construction of the Glasgow Central Railway was a huge engineering achievement. It began in 1890, long after Glasgow was built up, so it required enormous skill and confidence. The route followed the line of existing streets, like Argyle Street, and the tunnels were created by digging down to the depth where the tunnel roof could be formed. The surface was then reinstated while excavation, and shoring up to prevent collapse, continued under the roof. Buildings were underpinned to ensure their stability, sewers were remade and old culverted watercourses re-routed. It was a massive undertaking of a kind and a cost that would frighten lesser men, but in those days Glasgow's entrepreneurs thought and acted big. The line was fully opened in 1896 and although it was closed in 1964 the section through Anderston was reopened in the late 1970s. By that time Anderston Cross had gone, so the station was just called Anderston.

The south-facing side of Argyle Street is again bathed in sunshine, but the wheel has gone full circle and a bus is once more the centre of the picture, having taken over from the previously omnipresent trams. The No. 64 bus was in fact a direct replacement for the No. 9 tram, one of the principal routes along Argyle Street (see page 41). On the extreme right of the picture is a sign pointing to the Belfast Steamers. These ships of the Burns & Laird Line left from Lancefield Quay at the foot of Clyde Street and offered an overnight service from city centre to city centre. The last ships on the route, the *Royal Scotsman* and *Royal Ulsterman*, came on to the service in 1936 and ceased operations in October 1968. People who could afford a cabin slept in a bunk, while others sat in the lounge, or, if there was room, lay on the benches and tried to get some sleep. This was not easy if fellow passengers were determined to enjoy the crossing with the aid of drink and song. Anyone could join the party, but it was sometimes easier to get a quiet night on the deck, whatever the weather!

Says I, 'My lassie, where are ye going,
What do ye do by the Broomielaw?'
Says she, 'Kind sir, I'm a bleacher lassie,
In Cochrane's bleachfields on Kelvinhaugh.'

Bishop Street led north from Anderston Cross to St Vincent Street, passing through an underpass at Bothwell Street, which can be seen in the distance. In earlier times the street was known for the textile industry. James Monteith's weaving mill was established here in 1750 and about twenty years later it produced the first muslin made in Scotland. Another Bishop Street mill and bleachworks, operated by R. S. Cochrane, achieved lasting fame in the ballad *The Bleacher Lass of Kelvinhaugh*. The song treads the familiar path of boy meets girl, she spurns his advances, he persists, she relents, they marry and open a pub. The ending may be slightly at variance with the 'lived happily ever after' convention, but it is the second verse (see above) that excites because of its unusually specific reference to an actual industry.

McAlpine Street, seen here in a picture thought to date from 1906, was popularly regarded as being in Anderston, although it was just on the Glasgow side of the boundary. It was named after Angus McAlpine, the second provost of the burgh, who held office in 1832–3. He was a partner in Brown, Carrick & Company's bleachfield: the neighbouring Brown and Carrick Streets were named after the other partners. West College Street ran at right angles to the three streets, and its junction with McAlpine Street is seen here on the left. The central building is where Henry Alexander and Alexander Fergusson started making lead sheet and pipes in 1854. Alexander, Fergusson & Company, as they were known, later produced lead oxides, white lead and paste paints, and in 1874 moved this side of the business to Ruchill Wharf beside the Forth and Clyde Canal, while continuing to make other lead products and putty at McAlpine Street. Just out of the picture on the right was Anderston's first model lodging house – a place where homeless men could stay. A number of other such homes for men and women were also opened in the area, making it something of a gathering place for these unfortunate people.

The land running south from Stobcross Street to the river was originally divided into long, rectangular private estates, but these were quickly swamped by industry. Between them ran narrow streets, four of which had names apparently borrowed from London: Piccadilly Street (in the upper picture), Cheapside Street (lower picture), Hydepark Street and Whitehall Street. As development accelerated through the nineteenth century some housing was built at the north end of each street, but nearer to the docks every available patch of land was taken up by a huge variety of works and warehouses. It became a heavily congested 'hive of industry', but that and the nature of some of those businesses also made it a hazardous place to be when fire broke out, as it did in May 1912. The blaze destroyed a three-storey brick building running between Piccadilly and Clyde Streets. It was used by one company engaged in covering steam pipes and boilers, and another who made and sold cork products. The fire also threatened a wool broker, an oil merchant, a cooperage and a marine store, and endangered a bonded warehouse on the other side of Clyde Street. Fire also destroyed a whisky bond in Cheapside Street in March 1960 in a blaze that became world news when an unexpected explosion blew the front and back walls out of the building, killing fourteen fire-fighters and five men of the Salvage Corps, who were having to work dangerously close to the building in the narrow confines of Cheapside and Warroch Streets. It was all so different at the start of the nineteenth century when Henry Houldsworth set up the Anderston Cotton Works in Cheapside Street. The Houldsworths were leading figures in Anderston: Henry was the burgh's first provost and his son John, the last. They were also tough business people who saw early on that cotton had little future and moved into the nineteenth century's growth industries of iron and coal, starting with a foundry in Cheapside Street in 1823. Their huge six-storey works, built of brick and iron to make it 'fireproof', became a bonded warehouse in 1878 – directly opposite the one that burned down so disastrously in 1960. On the left of the Cheapside Street picture is St Mark's Church of Scotland.

With Harland & Wolff's Lancefield Street engine works in the foreground, this 1950s view shows the congested dockside area with the Cheapside Street bonded store and Houldsworth's mill ringed. *Inset*: A token of the Anderston cotton works.

When Anderston Cross and the streets to the north and south of it disappeared to make way for the motorway, Stobcross Street, seen here looking west from Anderston Cross, was demolished to create the route for the Clydeside Expressway. Its present incarnation as a fast dual-carriageway road is a far cry from the street's origins as the driveway to Stobcross House, a modest late seventeenth-century mansion built in the Scots vernacular style and inhabited by the Anderson family until John Orr of Barrowfield bought it in 1735. Although the quality of this picture is poor, the image of the fine, turreted tenement blocks on the left is strong enough to show just what Glasgow lost when it embarked on the wholesale demolition of areas like Anderston. The blocks are separated by Piccadilly, Cheapside and Warroch Streets respectively. The shop front on the extreme left-hand edge was on the corner of Clyde Street and was where the Anderston and District Health Association was set up in 1906 (see page 23).

Stobcross Street, Anderston

Stobcross Street is seen here looking east to Anderston Cross, where the two-storey station building can be seen in the distant centre of the picture. None of the buildings seen here remain standing, yet this bit of Stobcross Street has a claim to fame that has stirred the pride of Glaswegians for generations. On the right of the picture, just to the left of the lamp standard, is the first store opened in Glasgow by Thomas (later Sir Thomas) Lipton, in 1871. Its proximity to where the Irish boats came in allowed him to import butter, ham and other produce, which he marketed in a highly entrepreneurial way. From this one shop he went on to own a chain of grocery shops and a large store in Lancefield Street. He was a millionaire by the age of 30 and used this personal fortune to compete for the prestigious yachting trophy, the America's Cup. His yachts were always named *Shamrock*, which reflected his Irish origins, but not that nation's legendary luck because, although he tried five times, he never won. The dress shop on the left-hand edge of the picture was on the corner of McIntyre Street.

On the left of this view of Argyle Street, looking west from Anderston Cross, is the Gaiety Theatre with its canopy over the street and overhead gas lighting. Originally a warehouse, it became a music hall in 1893 and, in January 1899, the Tivoli Theatre. Its popularity waned in the face of competition from the movies and in 1907 it was sold and renamed the Gaiety. It showed films and hosted variety acts until 1935, when it became a full-time cinema. It would no doubt have ended as that, but in 1963 St Andrew's Halls burned down, leaving the Scottish National Orchestra without a home, so they moved into the old Gaiety, giving it a splendid late lease of cultural life amidst the decay and demolition. During the Gaiety's conversion an upright piano, possibly the one used to accompany the old silent films, was wheeled away up Argyle Street, manhandled up four flights of tenement stairs and into a top-floor flat, where it was turned into a cocktail bar. Very few of the buildings that once lined this section of Argyle Street have survived, although one that did, part way up on the right-hand side of the picture, housed the Shandon Bells pub, which became one of the city's top restaurants, the Buttery.

McIntyre Street was a couple of blocks to the west of Anderston Cross. It was lined with tenements, but was also graced by the library, which is on the left of this view looking towards Argyle Street from Stobcross Street. Occupying the centre of the street is a good piece of dating evidence for the twelve poorly printed old postcards included in this book. It is a horse-drawn van belonging to the Glasgow & South Western Railway, a company that ceased to exist in 1923, when it was absorbed into the London Midland & Scottish Railway (LMS). The company identifications on vehicles such as this would probably have been removed by the mid-1920s. The buildings here have also now gone, but McIntyre Street still exists, as the most easterly of the north–south aligned streets to have survived from the 1960s. Now a cul-de-sac, cut off from the fast carriageways of Stobcross Street, it bears no resemblance to this picture – even the buildings in Argyle Street, facing the camera, have gone, leaving a view through to St Vincent Street.

Hydepark Street, Anderston

The top end of Hydepark Street, seen here, between Stobcross and Argyle Streets, was known locally as wee Hydepark Street. It was domestic in character, while the longer section of the street running down to the river was more industrial. Like the neighbouring streets it was no stranger to fire. In April 1912 W. P. Lowrie's cooperage at No. 103 was partly destroyed by a blaze which burned merrily among the oak staves stacked ready to be made into barrels. The Hydepark name, initially used for a mansion house built by bleachers named McIlwham, became more widely known when an industry left the area taking the name with it. The firm of Mitchell & Neilson started making static steam engines at their Hydepark Foundry in 1836, but 24 years later the company was trading under the name Neilson & Company and making locomotives. It had also outgrown Anderston and in 1860–61 moved to Springburn and opened the Hydepark Locomotive Works.

Bakeries and flour mills were one of the area's major industries. One of the biggest was the Hydepark Bakery, set up in Hydepark Street around 1881 by the four Bilsland brothers. They continued to expand the business well into the twentieth century, by which time Bilsland's bread and rolls were amongst the best known and most popular in Glasgow. Two of their vans, made by Albion Motors in 1914, are seen here beside Scotstoun Showground. One of the Bilsland brothers, William, was elected to the town council for Anderston Ward in 1886 and became Lord Provost of Glasgow in 1906. During his time in office he worked to establish a dispensary on the corner of Clyde and Stobcross Streets, despite opposition from the medical profession which feared it would compromise existing services. Known as the Anderston and District Health Association, it dealt primarily with women's health, and infant and childhood diseases.

On the right of this view looking east along Argyle Street is its junction with Hydepark Street and Cranston Street, and beyond that, St Mark's Church. It was built as a Free Church in 1850 by people who broke away from St Mark's Church of Scotland congregation in Cheapside Street in 1843, at the time of a major split in church ranks known as the Disruption. It led to a proliferation of churches throughout Scotland, adding to the various Secession Churches created after earlier splits in church ranks. The rifts began to heal in 1900 when the breakaway churches came together as the United Free Church, which in turn reunited with the Church of Scotland in 1929. St Mark's became known as St Mark's West and then St Mark's Lancefield when it amalgamated with Lancefield United Free Church two years later. The building was demolished in 1969, the year after the amalgamated congregations of St Mark's, Anderston Old and Anderston St Peter's had moved into the new Anderston Parish Church. On the left-hand edge of the picture is the West Branch of the Savings Bank of Glasgow, the only building in the old Argyle Street to have survived, other than the Buttery.

The Savings Bank of Glasgow was set up in 1836 as the National Security Savings Bank. It was intended to provide a savings facility for people who could not afford the large sums required as deposits by large commercial banks. The bank's first branch in Anderston was opened in 1856, but closed the following year when two commercial banks offered savings facilities. A new branch, known as the West Branch, was opened in 1871. It was one of four that ringed the city centre and resulted in a significant increase in new depositors, many of whom were schoolchildren encouraged to develop the habit of thrift. Such was the success of the West Branch that it was replaced in 1900 with a superb red sandstone structure built to the designs of architect James Salmon and decorated in the art nouveau style for which Glasgow is famous. It closed in 1975, but remained standing thanks to a campaign to save it from demolition. It is thus one of the finest surviving art nouveau buildings in a city renowned for architecture of the period, but its location means that you are unlikely to find it in a tourist brochure!

With little space to kick a ball around, many youngsters sought sporting fame in the ranks of the Anderston Boxing Club, which met in a pend off Argyle Street. The lads in this picture certainly had some heroes to emulate. Jackie Paterson, a southpaw who joined the club as a boy in 1933, won the British flyweight championship six years later and continued to win titles until 1946 when he was World, Commonwealth and British champion at flyweight and Commonwealth and European bantamweight champion. He inspired another fighter, Peter Keenan, who although born in Scotstoun, boxed under the Anderston banner. Highly regarded in the sport as a boxer, not a slugger, he won the British and European bantamweight titles in May and September 1951, but failed in his bid for the world crown in South Africa, where he was fighting at altitude. When he retired from the ring Peter Keenan went on to act as promoter, with many of his boxing and wrestling shows being put on at the Kelvin Arena in Argyle Street.

Hill Street is seen here looking from Stobcross Street to Argyle Street and Elderslie Street beyond. The steep slope revealed by this picture makes the street name obvious, but with more than one Hill Street in Glasgow, the name of this one at Cranstonhill was changed in the late 1920s to Guest Street. St Patrick's, the first Catholic Church in the area, can be seen on the left. It was built in 1850 and there was a school alongside. Further up Hill Street, on the corner with Cranston Street, was the Cranstonhill United Free Church. It ceased to be used for worship in the late 1950s or early 1960s, but before demolition it got an extended lease of life when it was taken over by Associated Displays, who used it to construct television scenery and exhibition stands. Its height inside, plus the convenient location for the Kelvin Hall and BBC Scotland, made it ideal for these purposes.

OH, CRUMBS!

Oh! Jack—It's not Stevenson's

BUT———

THERE'LL BE NO CRUMBS
IF THE BREAD IS BAKED
by

STEVENSON

For a while there was a large gap site in Argyle Street between Belch Place, on the corner of Elderslie Street, and four tenements known as Lorne Place which sat between Elderslie and St Vincent Streets. This space was filled in the 1870s with three large tenement blocks, which included this little shop. The piecemeal development of the street probably explains why it was initially listed as 24$\frac{1}{2}$ Dumbarton Road, becoming 816 Argyle Street when the street name changed in 1906. The woman at the door is thought to be Mary Mills, one of three sisters. She remained unmarried and appears to have been the last member of the Mills family, which seem to have run the shop from the time it was built up to 1924, gaining along the way their self-proclaimed fame for soda scones and potted meats. Such items are not big sellers today, but they were sought after in the days when people had to make what little money they had go a long way! Good value for money is also the theme of J. & B. Stevenson's advertisement. Their Cranstonhill Bakery, a huge red and white brick building erected in Cranston Street around 1878, was latterly used by William Beattie as a biscuit bakery and demolished in 1969.

ELDERSLIE STREET, GLASGOW FROM ARGYLE STREET

Belch Place, the large tenement block on the left, was another fine-looking corner block with flats on the upper floors and an imposing frontage for the Clydesdale Bank at ground level. This junction of Argyle Street with Elderslie Street to the north and Hill Street to the south was originally known as Peden Cross, after the prophet who predicted that this would one day be the site of the cross of Glasgow. Sadly such optimism has evaporated and there is little about it now to warrant any name. The buildings have gone and the remaining cut-off rump of Argyle Street looks forlorn and deserted (and has emptied further with the introduction of parking meters!). Sandwiched between the striped awnings in the block on the opposite side of Elderslie Street is a close that gave access to the pawnbroker on the first floor – pawnbrokers were often located in premises above street level to give clients some degree of privacy. Next to it is Murdoch McLeod's dairy and alongside, partly hidden by the awning, is George Guthrie's butcher's business.

With the junction of Argyle Street and St Vincent Street now just a bend in the road, it is hard to appreciate that this was once a gushet junction with a prominent church in the angle formed by the two streets. The church was built as Anderston Parish Church in 1865 for a congregation that had its origins in a church at the foot of Clyde Street. The minister and most of the congregation went to the Free Church at the time of the Disruption in 1843, but some remained faithful to the established church and although the Clyde Street Church was destroyed by fire in 1849, they persevered and eventually amassed sufficient funds to build their new church. Adorning the entrance was a bust of Dr John Love, who had been the first minister of the Clyde Street Church and whose support for the work of the Glasgow Missionary Society led to the town of Lovedale in South Africa being named after him. The church became Anderston St Martin's when the free and established churches reunited in 1929, but appears to have dropped St Martin from the name, becoming Anderston St Peter's, when the congregation united with St Peter's Church, Brown Street, in 1951.

ARGYLE ST LOOKING EAST FROM FINNIESTON CROSS GLASGOW.

Anderston Parish Church can be seen tucked in behind the tenements in the centre of this picture looking east along Argyle Street. On the left is the junction with Claremont Street, with the seemingly inevitable pub on the corner, although one that has since become a dentist's surgery. The trend has gone the other way on the corner on the extreme left of the picture, where John Couper's drapery has now become a pub. Across Argyle Street, a sign for the Finnieston Dairy can be seen projecting from the building. The dairy's owner, Alex Brown, lived within sight of the shop, in Claremont Street. The run of buildings where the dairy was situated has been demolished and the site is now occupied by Cranstonhill Police Station. It was built as part of the area's redevelopment to replace the former police station on the corner of Lancefield and Cranston Streets.

The Education Act of 1872 made it compulsory for all children between the ages of five and thirteen to attend school. Prior to that churches had run schools as part of their parish responsibilities, but while some of these were good, provision was patchy and did not reach all children; the poorest were often the ones who missed out. Although the School Board, which was set up under the provisions of the Act, inherited the old school properties, they could not accommodate all the children and new schools were needed. One of these was Finnieston School, erected on a site bounded by Stobcross, Port, Cranston and Elliot Streets, which opened 1898. It was big, as these schools usually were, and in common with others in the city, it had no cloakroom, because the School Board reckoned that parents in poor districts would be unable to afford coats for their children. The boys of this class of 1949 are not badly dressed, although the variety of clothing reflects the less than wealthy backgrounds the boys came from. The school closed in 1970.

Below: Kent Road was one of five schools built around the city by the School Board to provide Higher Grade education for children whose parents could not afford to send them to established schools, like the High School, which charged higher fees. It opened in 1886, close to the junction of Kent Road and Argyle Street, in an area that the Board regarded as one that might provide a large number of pupils, but fewer children enrolled than had been hoped for, despite an emphasis being placed on subjects like science. As a result the school was scaled back after 1914 and any pupil wanting to go beyond third year had to go elsewhere. The building was replaced by the new Woodside Secondary School in 1968 and, when Finnieston Secondary closed, it became the principal school for the area. It took on a new role at the start of the 2006/07 session as the Glasgow Gaelic School, where all subjects are taught in the Gaelic language to children aged three to eighteen.

Right: The handsome memorial erected to the boys of Kent Road School who died during the First World War.

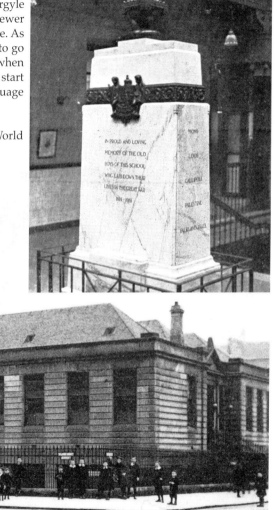

These fine terminal blocks are part of an architectural scheme of such high quality it would have rivalled the best of any city. The one on the right was built as Minerva Place and stands at the end of Minerva Street, which can be seen curving through the centre of the picture. The left-hand block, which ran round from Minerva Street to Finnieston Street, was known as Napier Place. It has long since been demolished and the site is now a car park for a small trading estate. It is difficult to be precise about when the picture was taken, although it must pre-date 1873, when tram rails were laid along Argyle Street in the foreground. The buildings were erected in the 1850s and are part of a larger scheme, the principal surviving element of which is St Vincent Crescent, a superb sweeping structure built in 1849–58 to the designs of architect Alexander Kirkland. Corunna Street, which links the crescent with Argyle Street, was completed at the same time. These elegant buildings offer a tantalising sense of what Finnieston might have been before the inexorable march of industry and commerce crowded it out.

The junction of Finnieston, Minerva and Argyle Streets was known as Finnieston Cross and is seen here in this view of Argyle Street with Minerva Place on the left. The angled junction with Kent Road can be seen in the centre of the picture. This left a triangular corner plot, which, unusually, was not filled by a striking building, but instead left an awkward gap in the Argyle Street frontage. This was filled by the run of small single-storey shops which can be seen behind the lighting standards on the right. These were occupied at the time this picture was taken by a rich diversity of small traders, like Mrs McCormack, who sold fancy goods, Miss Winton, a stationer, W. M. Bennett, a hatter and hosier, and boot maker Mrs J. Mill, who also had a shop on the corner of Bishop Street. Some of the neighbouring shops were occupied by grocer James Robertson, chemist and pharmacist James Manuel, James Martin, a tobacconist and cigar merchant, and jeweller and optician Anton Pfaff.

WIRELESS SETS from £3 : 17 : 6 complete.
GRAMOPHONES from £1 : 5 : 0. Accredited Agents for His Master's Voice, Columbia, Regal, and Decca Companies.
ACCUMULATORS CHARGED. 2 v. 30 amp.—2½d. Over 30 amp.—4d. and 6d.

Large Selection of GAELIC and LINGUAPHON LANGUAGE RECORDS.
SPANISH, ITALIAN, GERMAN. ::: EVERY TITLE IN STOCK
REPAIRS—MODERATE TERMS.

THE CITY GRAMOPHONE CO.,
(Please Note New Address)
1066 ARGYLE STREET.

PUDDLEDUCK—
Splashproof for
Silk Stockings.
1/- per jar.

This little tobacconist's shop, squeezed into a tiny site at 1071 Argyle Street, appears to have been a short-lived affair. Its fortunes were probably affected by those of the adjacent Finnieston Station on the North British Railway Company's Glasgow City and District Railway. The line ran from Queen's Dock, where the company's Stobcross Branch terminated, and went underground to a new low level station at Queen Street. From there it carried on to link up with other tracks to the east of the city. Work began in 1883 and involved an expensive cut-and-cover operation to create the 750-yard-long Finnieston Tunnel. This ran along the length of Kent Road, where very tricky geological conditions were encountered. Trains were running by 1886, but the station at Finnieston, fronting on to Argyle Street, was unable to compete with the ever improving trams and it closed in 1917. The building continued to be used by small businesses until gutted by fire in 1993. The City Gramophone Company was a grand title for a small shop which flourished briefly on the other side of the street: this advertisement appeared in 1934.

This ceremonial parade, seen from Argyle Street, is heading up Kelvingrove Street to the opening of the Scottish Exhibition of Natural History, Art and Industry held in Kelvingrove Park in 1911. At the top of the street, on the left, is the spire of the United Free – formerly United Presbyterian – Church, which occupied a triangular site between Kelvingrove and Derby Streets. On the other side of Derby Street was the Finnieston Free Church, seen here in the view on the right, which was built in 1878–80 designed by architect James Sellars. Although outside what might be regarded as the Finnieston area, its origins are firmly within it, starting in the late 1840s when a Robert Dunlop opened a day school in Stobcross Street. Moving a few years later to Grace Street, the school developed into a mission church catering for adults as well as children. This congregation moved to a new building at the top of Finnieston Street in 1856 and just over twenty years later occupied their new church at the corner of Derby and Bentinck Streets. It amalgamated with Claremont Church in 1963 to become Kelvingrove Parish Church and in 1986 came together with the new Anderston Church to form the united congregation of Anderston Kelvingrove.

The distinctive block on the corner of Argyle Street and Kelvinhaugh Street has now been demolished down to ground-floor level. It was on the end of a very long tenement block known as Franklin Terrace, built about 1850. Another significant building on this corner, the Sandyford Church, was behind the photographer's left shoulder, and is throwing a distinctive shadow across the foreground cobbles. It was erected in 1854–56 to the designs of, among others, the noted Glasgow architect John Honeyman. It later amalgamated with the Henderson Church. The picture was certainly taken after 1900, when tram No. 902 was introduced to the city's system, although the best dating evidence is probably the sale notices in the windows of James Chalmers' piano and organ shop. This seems not to have lasted long and ceased to occupy the corner premises around 1907.

A later occupant of the shop on the corner of Argyle and Kelvinhaugh Streets was Simms Motor Units. This company had been established by Frederick Richard Simms, who originally set himself up as a consulting engineer in London, in 1890, and became one of the early automotive industry's greatest innovators. During his early career he moved from developing individual items to making whole vehicles and back to making just one product, the magneto, a device which was largely his invention. This highly specialised business collapsed in 1913, but later that year Simms was back, supplying a range of electrical components for cars. In 1920, as the company prospered, it moved to a former piano works at Finchley and in the same year opened the first branch outside London, at 1175 Argyle Street, Glasgow – oddly also in a former piano shop. The first day of trading, 1 January, was probably quiet, but the business was still going strong in the 1950s when this picture, looking towards Argyle Street and Derby Street, was taken. The company moved to Finnieston Street in the late 1950s and ten years later to the east side of the city.

A No. 9 tram trundles along Argyle Street between Minerva Street and Corunna Street in 1960. The only other traffic on the cobbled surface consists of a lorry, a bus, another tram, a few cars and a couple of confused pedestrians – somewhat less than is usual today. The former Kelvin Cinema can be seen in the background, above the tram's roof. It was huge, with 1,874 seats, and was designed by architects A. V. Gardner and W. R. Glen. It was opened in May 1930 and was remodelled six years later. The most distinctive external feature was a low octagonal tower on the eastern corner, while internally the screen was flanked by exotic scenes derived from Turkey and Spain – places people could only dream about in those days. Following closure in 1959 it became a sports arena, where Peter Keenan staged many of his promotions, and it was also used as a bingo club, nightclub and 'the world's largest Indian restaurant'. It has now been demolished and the site redeveloped. One surviving detail from this picture is Harvey's funeral parlour with its splendid square clock, just to the right of the tram's No. 9 route indicator.

The No. 9 was the last tram service in city, withdrawn in September 1962. The occasion was marked by a special procession and Glaswegians turned out in force to watch the famous old vehicles run into history. Youngsters put coins on the line to be squashed by tram wheels, as souvenirs. A little film was made using images of the No. 9 route to tell the story of the trams, their passengers and crews. The producer, Kevin Brownlow, called it *9 Dalmuir West*, but it was the other terminal, Auchenshuggle, that entered the country's folklore in a song – 'Shuggle, shuggle, shuggle up the road tae Auchenshuggle' – and as the home town of the cartoon character *Oor Wullie*. The Auchenshuggle tram is seen here passing the end of Lymburn Street on the right, with tracks going off to the left into Radnor Street, another tram destination. Beyond the van is another little bit of Glasgow's folk heritage, the Argyle Street tree – the only one along this stone-lined canyon.

In April 1859 a group of gentlemen gathered at a house in Kelvingrove Street with the intention of forming a bowling and curling club for people living in the vicinity of St Vincent Crescent. They had already obtained, from the Stobcross Estate, an offer of ground at the west end of the crescent, so their immediate task was to raise finance, recruit members and create the facility. This was done by June 1860 when the green was opened, to the accompaniment of music from the band of the 2nd Battalion, the Rifle Volunteers. After the initial lease the club was faced with a succession of short-term arrangements until 1906, when a new fifteen-year lease was obtained on a site further east along the terrace. This leasing arrangement continued until 1950, when the site was purchased. The curling element of the club apparently ceased in the 1870s and tennis, introduced in 1906, ended in the 1930s, but the St Vincent Bowling Club celebrated its centenary in 1959 and, at the time of writing, is heading for its 150th year in 2009. The picture shows the first green, with the magnificent sweep of St Vincent Crescent behind.

This staff photograph of the Stobcross Motor Company was probably taken in the late 1920s, soon after the business was set up in Galbraith Street, later renamed Minerva Street. The company also dealt in marine engines, but concentrated on motor vehicles, becoming the city's main agent for Jowett cars in the 1950s. Finnieston played a significant role in the development of automotive engineering in Scotland. The Albion Motor Car Company started life in 1899 at No. 169 Finnieston Street, before moving to Scotstoun as builders of commercial vehicles. George Halley set up his Glasgow Motor Lorry Company at the same premises in 1901 and in 1904 the Bergius Car and Engine Company moved in. They produced Kelvin Cars, later moving to Port Dundas, where they made marine engines. Carlaw's, one of the city's largest car dealerships and garages, was established in Finnieston Street in 1901 and continued to have a presence on the street for most of the century. Major dealerships and small specialist garages still operate in the Finnieston area, maintaining a link with the industry's pioneering days.

Stobcross Station, like that at Anderston Cross, was on the Caledonian Railway's low level Glasgow Central Railway. This line also formed an underground junction with the company's line to and from Dunbartonshire just to the west of the station, so trains using that line also ran through Stobcross and Anderston. For all of its 60-plus years of operation prior to closure in 1964 the underground line was used by steam locomotives and, although the tracks briefly broke out of their subterranean confines at Stobcross, the platforms here, as at Anderston Cross, were gloomy, dirty and full of smoke. The railway company compensated for these Stygian caverns by constructing some very fine buildings on the surface, like that at Anderston Cross and the splendid Caledonian Mansions at Kelvinbridge, which still survives above the defunct section of line between Stobcross and Maryhill. When the Dunbartonshire line was reinstated in the late 1970s, it was with electric trains. The reopened, and now much cleaner, station at Stobcross was renamed Exhibition Centre, because of its proximity to the Scottish Exhibition and Conference Centre (SECC).

If the idea behind the Anderston Centre on Argyle Street was to replace houses and shops with something new, the Clydeway Industrial Centre was envisaged as a modern alternative to crumbling back-court workshops. Again the city fathers' pride knew no bounds as they welcomed the first decked industrial area in a British city. It was built in the mid-to-late 1960s to the designs of Jack Holmes & Partners at the junction of Finnieston Street and the new Clydeside Expressway, formerly Stobcross Street. Made predominantly of red brick and concrete, it was an uncompromisingly massive structure that somehow fitted in to the architectural landscape more favourably than some of the other developments of the time. In that sense it has stood the test of time, although it has since been rebranded as Skypark and remodelled as office, call centre and work space. 'Industry', a word once synonymous with Glasgow, has quietly been dropped.

Construction of Queen's Dock began in 1872 on the former Stobcross Estate of Anderston's founder, James Anderson. In all 2,850,000 tons of material was excavated from the 33.5 acre site to create a vast dock complex of two berthing basins, an outer basin and nearly two miles of quayside. Ships were using the dock by 1877, but construction continued until 1880, when the final coping stone was laid. It was inscribed 'This dock, by kind permission of Her Most Gracious Majesty Queen Victoria, named Queen's Dock'. Here a sailing vessel sits near the entrance of the outer basin, while a crane loads a railway truck of coal into one of three puffers, an operation that created clouds of coal dust and blackened anyone standing too close. The dock also handled general cargoes and ocean-going freighters, but the rapid decline in traditional shipping and the rise in bulk and containerised traffic resulted in the dock's closure at the end of 1969. Waste material from the vast programme of demolition that was going on around the city was then dumped in it and steadily the once vast docks were filled in. The Scottish Exhibition and Conference Centre was opened on the site in 1985.

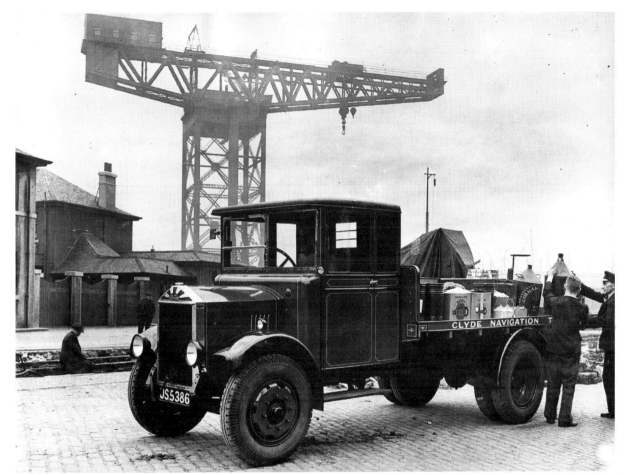

Dockside facilities had to be able to handle the heavy loads created by Glasgow's manufacturing industry, including steam railway locomotives. This challenge was initially met by a 130-ton capacity steam crane erected on Finnieston Quay in 1895, but the loads got bigger and it had to be replaced in 1932. The new crane on Stobcross Quay was, perhaps surprisingly, not the product of Glasgow's own engineering expertise, but was built by Cowans, Sheldon & Company of Carlisle. It had a 150-foot long hammerhead jib and was capable of lifting 175 tons. The Finnieston Crane wasn't just used for loading heavy items, but also for fitting out new ships. It was so distinctive it was adopted as the badge for Finnieston School and this strong image helped it to survive the cull of the 1960s and 70s. The crane has become something of an icon for the city rather than just a local symbol. It is seen here in 1934 behind an Albion lorry, which, like the crane, was owned by the Clyde Navigation Trust. The man on the left is working on the railway tracks into the docks.

The ferry competed for custom with the Harbour Tunnel, access to which was gained through distinctive domed rotundas; the south-side one is seen here from Finnieston, framed by the ferry superstructure. There were in fact three tunnels, two for wheeled vehicles and a smaller one for pedestrians. Excavation began in 1890 and the first traffic went under the river in 1895. The rotundas contained a stair for pedestrians and lifts for horses and carts. The privately owned and operated facility was not a commercial success and Glasgow Corporation had to provide financial support before taking it over in 1926. The vehicle tunnels were closed in 1943, but the pedestrian tunnel remained in use until 1980. It leaked, the floor was wet, well-spaced bulbs gave only a dim light and along one side a large pipe supported on blocks could have hidden anything or anyone. Add to this the sounds of persistent dripping and distant footfalls, and it was best to keep one's imagination in check when walking through the tunnel, yet it remains, for this writer anyway, a fond memory of old Glasgow. Since closure, the rotundas have had a variety of uses from ice-cream parlours to casinos.